Dedicated to my DH, DW & CW...

Dear Adventurers on the Path Less Texted,

As we once again venture into the wilderness of digital communication, we find ourselves on the brink of exploring its more... titillating territories. "WTH Does That Mean? Censored: A Cheeky Sexting Guide for Grown-Ups" is not your ordinary field guide. No, dear readers. It is a map to the hidden treasures and secret caverns of adult digital discourse, where emojis and acronyms dance together in a seductive ballet of bytes and bits.

If our first journey, "WTH Does That Mean?!," armed you with the essentials to navigate the bustling cities and towns of Gen Z lingo, consider this expedition your guided tour through the intriguing nightlife of those very locales. Here, the language is spicier, the symbols more suggestive, and the stakes amusingly higher.

Why, you might ask, should one venture into these steamy digital waters? Because, fellow Gen Xers, the art of flirtation and adult conversation has evolved. Gone are the days of passing notes in class or the nervous anticipation of a rotary phone call. Today, intrigue, charm, and even romance unfold on the screens of our smartphones, in a language punctuated by emojis and crafted with acronyms.

This guide is your decoder ring, a tool to unlock the mysteries of digital desire. It's a testament to our adaptability and proof that, even as the world changes, our human need for connection and fun remains constant.

So, whether you're a seasoned sexter or someone who's just curious, this book is for you. It's a celebration of our generation's resilience, a nod to our willingness to learn, and a chuckle at the absurdity of it all. We've mastered the mixtape, navigated the internet explosion, and now, we'll conquer the nuanced world of sexting with the same gusto.

Buckle up, dear readers. It's time to swipe right on learning, to double-tap into our adventurous spirit, and to send a wink emoji to the unknown. Welcome to "WTH Does That Mean? Censored." Your journey into the cheeky side of texting begins now.

With a sly smile and an open heart,

Jess x

P.S. Remember, the key to great digital flirtation is not just in what you say, but in the spaces you leave for the imagination.

TDTM

Talk Dirty To Me

RUH — Are You Horny?

GNOC — Get Naked on Camera

WTTP — Want To Trade Photos?

YPOM — Your Place Or Mine?

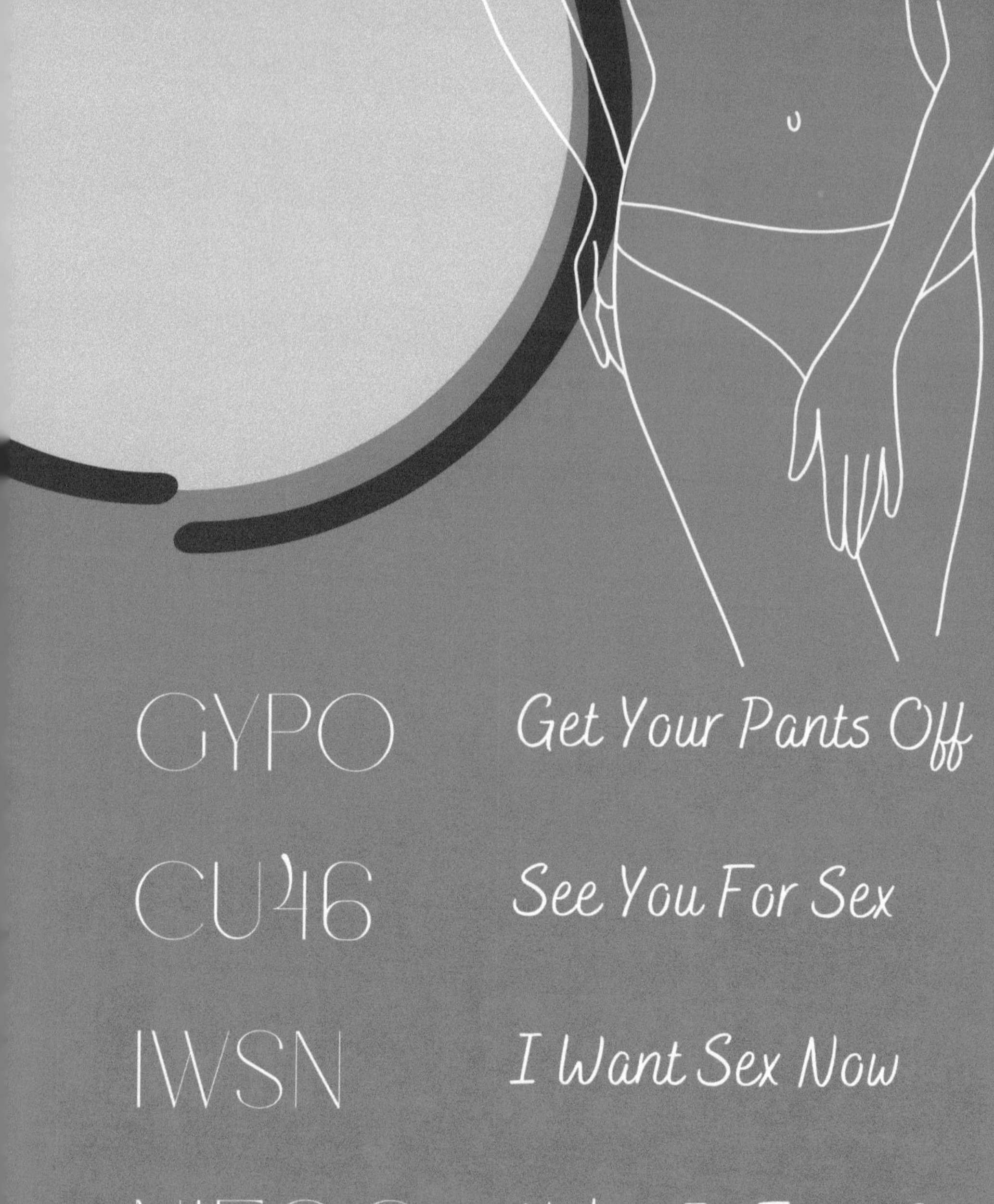

GYPO — Get Your Pants Off
CU46 — See You For Sex
IWSN — I Want Sex Now
NIFOC — Naked In Front Of Computer
BTM — Bow To Me

RMLAC   Ride Me Like A Cowboy
KOTL   Kiss On The Lips
H4Y   Hot For You
FB   F*** Buddy
DUM   Do You Masterbate?

KWSTA

Kiss With Serious Tongue Action

TMFB	Take Me From Behind
IIT	Is it Tight?
FMUTA	F*** Me Up The Arse
SOMF	Sit On My Face
IEZRU	I'm Easy, Are You?

HMTTBP

Handcuff Me To The Bed Post

WAP	Wet Ass Pussy
LB?W/C	Like Bondage? Whips or Chains?
WYSW	What's Your Safe Word
FMLTWIA	F*** Me Like The Whore I Am

DYSL

Do You Scream Loud?

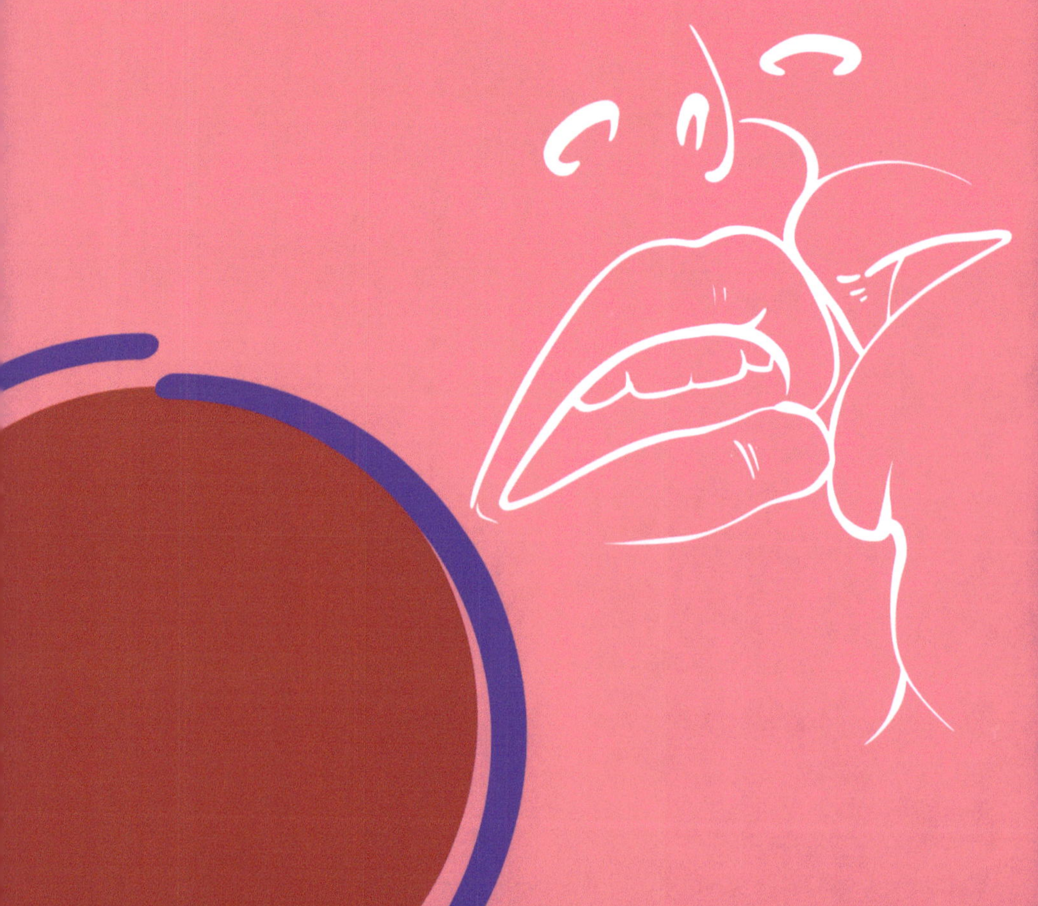

IAYM	I Am Your Master
Q2C	Quick To Cum
SMN	Scream My Name
SOMOIM	Spit On Me Or In Me
IKYWM	I Know You Want Me

MMSS	Make Me See Stars
PBDWBN	Princess By Day, Whore By Night
SMITOWIL	Spank Me It's The Only Way I'll Learn
YNASWM	Your Nudes Are Safe With Me

MILF

*Mother I'd Like To F****

**Can also be applied to Dads (DILF) and Grannies (GILF)!

STM	Spank The Monkey
FWB	Friends With Benefits
SMT	Suck My Tits
TMA	Tap My Arse

CMD

Choke Me Daddy

TMB	Tickle My Balls
TMU	Tie Me Up
GNRN	Get Naked Right Now
KITTY	Pussy
FMLTNT	F*** Me Like There's No Tomorrow

FMF — F*** My Face

BOB — Battery Operated Boyfriend

MSNUW — Mini Skirt No Underwear

HFY — Hot For You

BMBNMH

Break My Bed Not My Heart

SMT	Suck My Toes
JEOMK	Just Ejaculated On My Keyboard
XTC	Ecstasy
TITB	Tonight I'm The Boss

PMH
Pull My Hair

FMN	F*** Me Now
WTTY	Want To Taste You
TMTIB4I	Tease Me Til I'm Begging For It
DBTTM	Do Bad Things To Me
BABGT	Been A Bad Girl Today

CTDOYWO

Close The Door On Your Way Out!